Snapchat:
Marketing Mastery for Beginners

Table of content:

Introduction: Cornering the Market

No matter what it is that you are doing you have to know your market; you have to understand your target audience. Snapchat is mostly used by a younger demographic. Having that said, if you are trying to market for AARP, snapchat may not be the best vehicle in which to do so. The largest age group to use snapchat is from 15 to 30 years old, although that number is rapidly expanding even as we speak.

You should also keep in mind that snapchat is a "mobile only" kind of application. This means that the only people likely to use snapchat are those that have smart phones. One other hurdle of snapchat when it comes to cornering your market is the fact that there is currently no way to search within the snapchat data banks for users.

Unlike Face Book, you can't just type someone's name into a search bar to find them. Snapchat makes things are just a little bit more interesting than that. Snapchat still relies heavily on cross media exposure as well as just simple vocal transmission from user to user. At its core snapchat is simply an online platform that allows you to use social media for quick videos, pictures, and messages to further your brand in the public sphere of influence.

It is all of these sent attachments that are referred to as "snaps". Once these snaps are sent the recipient of them will have a limited amount of time at your discretion to view the content before it is automatically deleted from the server. It's like sending a message with an expiration date. And the fact that those goofy photos and videos that you sent when you were drunk at the nightclub at 3 in the morning is one of the innovative aspects of snapchat that the younger crowd like so much about.

It seems they have learned from previous generations who used to post questionable things on Face Book only to have it come back and haunt them when they were trying to land a good job later in life. They were always told be careful what you post because *it's permanent.*

But with the "use once and destroy" model of snapchat, folks don't have to worry about that anymore! They can send out as many disposable messages, pictures, and videos as they want. This is why over two thirds of all college students are using this platform to express themselves with their friends. So now that you know your market. You better get to work!

Chapter 1: Five Fundamentals of Snapchat for Business

Having good business acumen with Snapchat is like having some good common sense. As long as you are able to follow basic fundamental standards and rules, you will succeed. So here they are for you folks, the five fundamentals of snapchat for business!

Use in Store Coupons

Everyone's loves a good discount, and everyone loves a good coupon. In fact, nothing gets a potential followers attention more than a good coupon. This will generate interest, and bring people to your brand. It doesn't necessarily matter what kind of in store coupons you use to promote your business, just make sure that you use them.

Recent polls have actually confirmed that over 50% of users are in fact more likely to take part of your goods or services if you preface them with a good in store coupon. I can remember the first time that I used one of these in store coupons with my own business. I had tried a few things that didn't work so well, so I figured that it couldn't hurt to give I story coupons a try.

Well, it seemed like the very second I put my coupons out there; massive amounts of attention were drawn in my product's direction. It's amazing what a few discounts can do for your bottom line. Don't be afraid to offer up some goodies in order to get a good audience for your craft.

I had been struggling to make any headway at the time when a friend had suggested that I give these coupon based incentives a try. I saw a difference quite literally overnight, as my hits started to increase exponentially by the early hours of the morning. So get ready to see the traffic to your sight increase exponentially, and get out those coupons! It's worth it!

Look Out for New Product Announcements

I have an announcement to make guys! If you really keep your eyes peeled for the hottest new trends on the market you can then make them part and parcel to your snapchat campaign! You can always get the word out to your follower through new product announcements. This is a fundamental aspect of snapchat and it's not going to go away any time soon. There are just too many ways that you can make your product announcements good for your business to pass up.

You can make your snapchat platform like your own personal billboard that announces exactly what you need to do and how you need to do it. Set up this announcement in a strategic place that helps you connect with your own personal target groups. Once you do this, all of the rest will follow! Always be vigilant and always be on the look out for any and all new potential opportunities for new product announcements! It really works!

Take a Look Behind the Scenes

Whether it's their favorite movie, or a brand new car design never before released, everyone likes a little sneak peek behind the scene right? Letting your followers look behind the scenes at your product should be a given. It's like you are able to give them a chance to try on new clothes just to see if they fit! Just think about it, no one likes to go to the store and purchase something that ends up not working out for them!

This is the uncertainty that breeds hesitance in the first place! In order to cut through all of this, you can give your clients a sneak peek instead! The more you can inundate your followers into what it is that you do, the happier everyone will be! So make sure you always allow for a good look behind the scenes! This is a great opportunity for you. Think of it as open house in which you can show your followers—and by extensions the world—just what you have to offer. Don't miss out on this great and amazing opportunity!

Use Time Limited Promos and Deals

I just can't stress enough how important this is! The more that you use the time limited promos the more you can count on having customers! There has to be a bit of a showman in all of us, a bit of a carnival barker extraordinaire! And it's always these time limited promos and deals that help us to bring that out of us! It's just marketing 101 folks!

There is just something about putting a time limit on something that makes people set the date on their calendar and get ready to shop before the time limit runs out. If you have a sale that lasts until Saturday, you will invariably have a bunch of folks showing up at the very last minute of Saturday to check out your wares. This is where your limited time promos and deals should come around to draw them in.

These promos can do you a whole world of good. There are many other multifaceted strategies that you could utilize in this vein as well. If you can have a limited time only, half off sale, you can start a promotional offer of free shipping and handling, you name it, and you can do it! But only for a limited time (Sorry, just had to throw that one in there)!

Use Freebies and Giveaway Incentives to Build your Base

Who likes to get stuff for free? Just about every single person on the planet called Earth! Just like the above mentioned promos ad deals, giveaways and freebies go with the territory when it comes to reinvigorating your base. This doesn't mean that you want to give away the whole store, there are certain things by principle that you just shouldn't give away. Incentives are meant to be a net plus for your business not a net loss!

But having that said, you do want to make sure that you are able to incentivize your followers to jump on board your team for whatever it is that you are wishing to sell or promote! Just flesh out a working incentive based strategy and the rest of it will fall in place accordingly. It works every time folks! Just follow the fundamentals of it, and you will do just fine!

Chapter 2: Marketing Through Snapchat

There are several ways you can market your business through snapchat, this chapter highlights only a few of the most effective. In the end this is just a template for you to follow, you will have to experiment on your own and find exactly what works best for you.

Use Snapchat to Provide Access to Live Events

Regular use of the social media platform known as "snapchat", works to greatly streamline the ease of access with which you can provide content that is streamed as a live event. You can use snapchat to achieve quite a bit in this arena! This content can then be used for finding an appropriate product launch date, and unique promotional events such as rewarding the 100th person to buy your product.

The National Basketball Association for example, has used snapchat in several ways, such as in the promotion of games, and even the marketing of merchandise and other memorabilia. There is never a game that goes by without a snap or two sent their fans way. All in all, when you use snapchat to provide you with access to live events, it is a win-win situation. There are no complaints there! You should definitely give it a try. So yes, make sure to use snapchat to provide access to new and exciting live events.

Use Snapchat for Private Content

Snapchat can work as a great filter for all of your private content. Using private filters are especially useful for delivering tailor made information to specific groups, in order to excite that specific part of the online community. It's a way to make your followers feel like they are on the cutting edge of your promotions. If you want them to feel like hey are part of something new, bold, and exciting, you can use snapchat to do it.

This very method has been used for example with fashion brands such as Michael Kors, and Rebecca Minkoff, as well as Victoria's Secret. There is an endless array of companies and brands that have benefited from this feature. All of these companies have been able to tip off their fans about high end new clothing they have developed, before their general release date. Likewise, you should be able to use snapchat to do the same with your own fan base.

Network with Influencers

Life is all about networking. And of course, networking is a key aspect of any business relationship, and this couldn't be more true than with snapchat. When you partner with "influencers", with people who already have a heavy social media footprint, you are able to throw your weight around much more than you would if you did not. These veterans of snapchat no doubt have many finely honed skills of the trade such as excellent video content at their disposal that can greatly boost your disposition as well. It never hurts to network with some good and knowledgeable influencers.

Support Social Media Account Takeovers

This is a takeover! And no it's not unheard of. There are several instances in which users have allowed other snapchat users to take over their account, so that they can help them gain more followers. This goes right along the lines of the above mentioned section of networking with influencers. Don't be shy of these guys, and make them your best friends, because if you scratch their back, they will scratch yours!

So if you know a heavy hitter in the business and they are willing to take your snapchat hat for a ride, by all means, let them do it! Rather than have some internet hijacker take over your account, let these seasoned pros lead you to success! These are the social media account takeovers of the good kind and you should to your best to support them! It's like taking someone who is an expert driver and handing them the wheel of your jalopy! If you believe they can get you there, hand them the keys ad let them get your motor running!

Share Your Promo Codes

It always pays to share your Promo Codes. Just take the example of the frozen yogurt chain 16 handles. They used snapchat with stunning success. They were able to make use of snapchat's instantaneous picture app, and used it to create a massive amount of interest in their product. If anyone was following this company they automatically got a promo code that would get them special deals and discounts. It's a shopping spree just waiting to happen!

Just think about the last time you felt excited to be invited to a great promotional sale at your favorite store, this is exactly how your followers will feel as well. It's like an addictive compulsion, and once you send these promo codes their way, they can not resist it! They will get that same thrill of excitement and feel compelled to check out your merchandise. This is what marketing is all about! So make sure that you share your Promo Codes!

Grant VIP Access

If you want to make your follower feel special you should periodically grant them VIP access. Being able to grant them instant VIP access does more than make them feel special however, it breaks down barriers. Just think, in the past major name brads had to wait weeks, sometimes months, in order to send samples of their material to potential consumers.

But now you can send your followers access with just the simple click of your mouse! So go ahead and get the word out and make them feel like a VIP! The better they feel the better your own bottom line will be! Go ahead and grant VIP access! Your very important people will thank you for it in the end! And as you see the results, you will have to thank yourself as well!

<u>Be Sure to Feature Your Followers</u>

It's always good to give a mention to your followers, and snapchat allows you just the opportunity to do just that. This is what GrubHub did, this online food service was able to really clean up just by featuring their followers. Imagine what you could do by doing the same exact thing!

Learn from them. When you feature your own followers with snapchat you can use your own weekly content, create tailor made promotional tours, and more! So be sure to always feature your followers! They only know what you tell them, so be sure to tell them a lot! It's not rocket science folks! Just feature your fan base and you will be in great shape!

Chapter 3: Knowing the Rules of Snapchat

Everything has rules, it just might not always be spelled out, but in this chapter you will find the basic rules of snapchat. Follow them closely and apply them to your everyday experience with snapchat! The better you know the rules the better your business will be!

Be Authentic

Have you ever been put off by someone that you found to be incredibly inauthentic? Did you cringe as they seemed to be just going through the motions halfheartedly? No one likes fake sentiment and false enthusiasm. It's like your mom told you on your first day of elementary school; just be yourself! It's pointless to try and be anyone else!

And people can smell a phony a mile away! The whole purpose of snapchat is to be able to tell the world about yourself, not to hold back. So take away all of your facades and pretenses and be authentic. Authenticity can score way more points than any slick promotional deal so just do your best to be yourself! This is a cardinal rule of snapchat! So be sure to remember it!

Create Memorable Material

If you don't remember it, then neither will anyone else! So make sure that you create memorable material. If you are promoting music, make every riff, and every beat count. If you are selling cheese make sure you put the best cheddar up front! It doesn't matter what you are doing, as a rule, make sure you make it count! Always create memorable material! Part and parcel to all this is creating a catchy slogan for your goods or services. Do you remember the phrase from the 1980's anti-drug campaign, "This is your brain on drugs, any questions?"

I bet even if you weren't even born in the 1980's you remember that one! That's how good it was—and that's the whole point—it was catchy! And the same should be said for your own slogans as well. If they can't remember it, then it probably wasn't worth remembering. Sorry folks, don't mean to be blunt, but it's the truth. People have bad memories nowadays, so if you would like to make stuff stick, you have to create content that is _memorable_ in the first place!

Use a Small Sample Group to Test Your Product

There is a reason why researchers find, locate, and utilize a sample group before they try something out on the larger population; it minimizes the impact of failure. Not only that, it gives you the chance to correct your course, and change the trajectory enough to ensure success the future time around. Snapchat allows you to test out your product on an audience in real time and then adjust it accordingly.

You can float out a trial balloon to a small group of your followers and if it goes over well you can then introduce it to further groups. But if it goes over like a *lead balloon* however, then you will be able to examine just what it was that had went wrong in the first place, and correct it. It really pays to use a small sample group to test your products. Put it out there, monitor the results and then adjust to what works and what does not work.

Keep a Record of Your Successes

You win some, and you lose some, who should keep count right? Well, if you want any measure of success, *you should keep count*. You should keep a record of all of your successes and list them for all of your followers to see. This is your built in testament as to what your goods or services can do for future clients. You need to make public every single benefit that was derived and use it to generate renewed interest in your chosen focal groups.

This is your living resume and points of references. As you build it your whole world will increase as a result. Always make sure you keep this living record updated. Build it up, and build it well. Not to quote from a famous movie or anything but, "Build it and they will come!"

Publish Content on a Daily Basis

Since the whole premise of snapchat is to have content that quickly evaporates after a 24 hour period, you need to get yourself into the habit of routinely adding new material. As soon as one article expires add another one. If you don't those pesky short attention spans of your followers will lose interest and they will move elsewhere. You need to keep something riveting and exciting going just about every 24 hour period.

Admittedly this can be hard on your own sometimes, but if that is the case, then you are in luck, because snapchat has an app for that! You should have what is called in snapchat parlance, a "flipbook" of all your important content so you can easily update your material. Make sure you make use of this tool directly provided by the snapchat app. It couldn't be easier. Publish content on a daily basis and they will never lose interest! That's it folks! And the rest is history in the making!

Chapter 4: Direct Benefits of Snapchat

When I speak of using snapchat for business the question most frequently asked of me is simply; how can I benefit from snapchat? They usually already have their own preconceived notions in place before they even ask, but I try to inform them in a non biased approach as best I can. So here goes nothing! I know you want to Snapchat! Just look at all of these great benefits!

You can Demo Your Products

There is no better platform than snapchat that enables you to demonstrate what your product is and what it can do. Take for example the case of Amazon's recent use of snapchat to demo the Amazon Echo. The folks at Amazon used snapchat in order to bring about greater awareness about Echo and its artificially intelligent voice, "Alexa".

This denizen of the world we call "Artificial Intelligence" has taken the world by storm, and it was with this promo that Amazon first galvanized public attention, and made the world take notice. It was an almost overnight success story and Jeff Beezos (the founder of Amazon) couldn't have been happier. Not only for himself but for the impact he made on the lives of consumers.

The end result of this highly publicized demo through snapchat was gaining over 6000 hits in just the first few moments of the demo! The first time that I tried this I was able to get hundreds of hits without even lifting a finger! Snapchat is a wonderful platform in which you can demo any product! It doesn't matter if you are using a temporary

You are Able to Address Relevant Topics

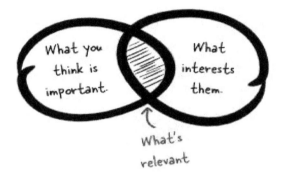

Snapchat gives you a platform like never before to address relevant topics in real time. And the power of this platform to change how people think about any given product or idea has been proven time and time again. Just take for example what happened recently with Dove Soap. That's right, that same old bar of soap hanging out in your bathroom soap dish has recently sparked an incredible debate on snapchat.

This rather innocuous brand of bar soap has been around for a long time, not much to change there right? Wrong. You see, although traditionally this brand was preferred by mid to elderly aged women, after a brief but effective snapchat campaign that involved just 30 women snapchatting over relevant topics with a team of psychologist and other experts, about body image and other self esteem issues relevant to young women.

This brief snap session created 75 unique chats that generated approximately 130,000 hits generating renewed interest in the age old standard of Dove Soap for a whole new (and younger) audience. All of this occurred simply because of the power of being able to address relevant topics in real time. It's certainly a breath of fresh are to be able to address real and relevant topics. It's like a "choose your own adventure" story on a deeply personal level; use snapchat to make these amazing connections with your base.

Snapchat is a Very Personal Platform

Snapchat is by far, one of the most personal social media platforms that you will ever find. You are able to tailor and customize every aspect of this social media outlet until it conforms to your exact specifications. You can make your Snapchat channel a one size fits all, or you can make it a completely specific experience for your target group of users. It's all up to you. Snapchat is a very personal platform and you should treat it as such. The more intimate your snaps the more of a following that you will have.

Snapchat works in Real time

This platform does exceptionally well in real time, and should be used as such. There is no end of the exciting narratives you can create on any given subject as it is transpiring. This is a great tool to have at your disposal when you are overseeing live events, because you are able to make the changes you need on the fly in real time. And just like that you can alter the entire course of a sales or information campaign.

I can clearly remember a time that a musician friend of mine was holding a benefit concert for a charity organization and he needed someone to coordinate what was going on in real time. Well, to make a long story short--he knew of my experience with snapchat and immediately recruited me for the cause. He knew that I had the experience to get the job done, and trusted me to come up with new and exciting ways to make a statement.

I was able to give all of his followers on his "go fund me" page a play by play of everything he and his band were doing, and by the end of the day this real time data translated into real life people donated to the charity. Its not by the seat of your pants, its by the speed of your computer processer, because snapchat most certainly does work in real time.

Conclusion: Getting the Word Out

In the game of marketing and advertising there are always going to be those that are able to get more out of any give platform than others. Some just have that special drive to dominate, and others just have such good products that they speak for themselves. But regardless, they all have something in common; they need to have tools to help accentuate what they already have. This is true across all common denominators, and it needs to be recognized as such.

I can still remember the first time that I even heard of snapchat. I thought it was the silliest thing, and like many others figured it was a fad that would quickly go away. Well here we are in 2017 and there is no sign of abatement any time soon. Now I realize the reasons for snapchat's staying power and they are ingenious. For the first time snapchat offers the internet a one stop shop in which they can dispose their left over multimedia.

The platform allows people to be themselves, communicate and express their interests, without having to worry about these expressions floating through the halls of cyberspace for all eternity. It is for all of these reasons and more that snapchat is going to be with us for quite a long time. So you better go ahead and get the word out! Snapchat is here to stay! Thank you for reading!